I0415076

This Book Belongs To:

____

BY
Home Planners And Journals

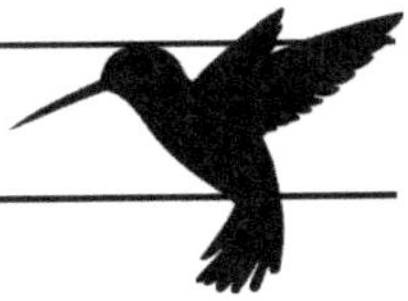

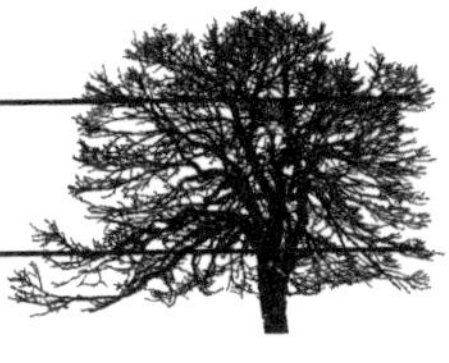

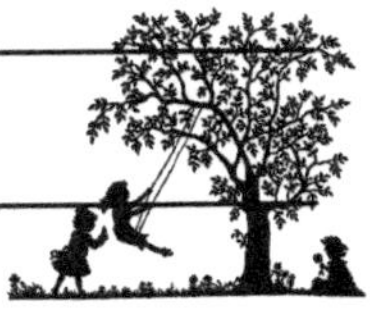

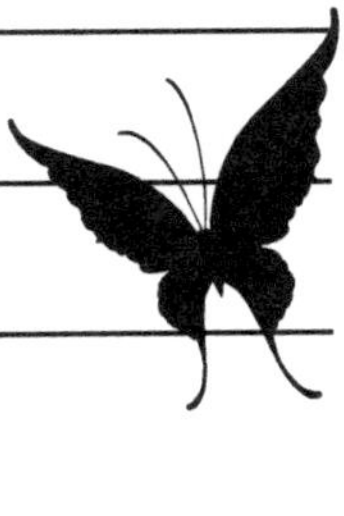

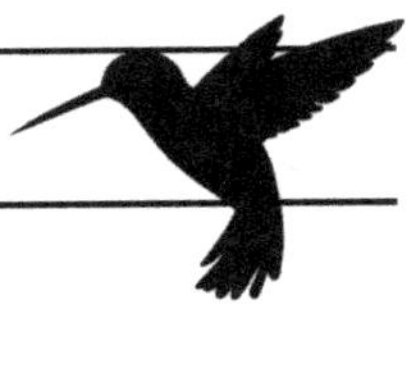

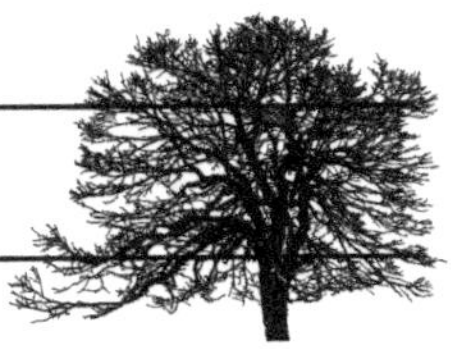

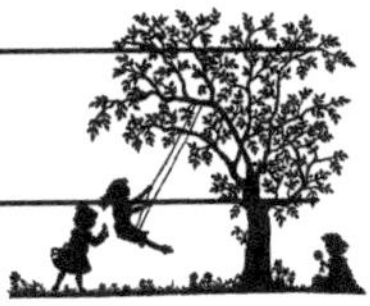

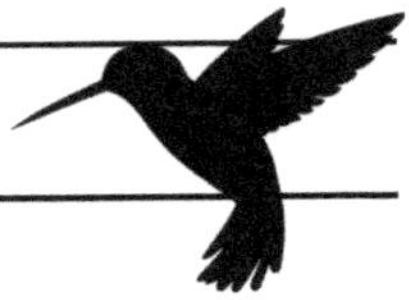

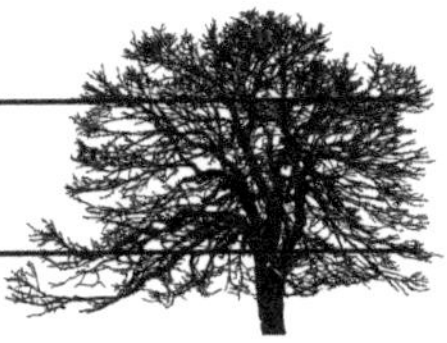

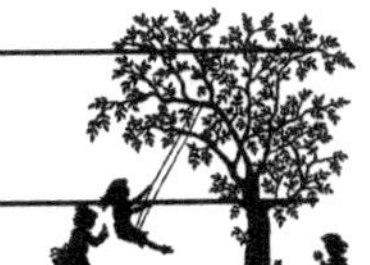

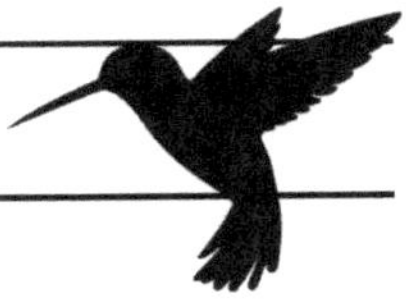

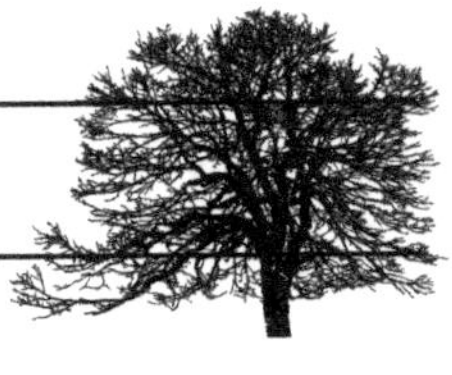

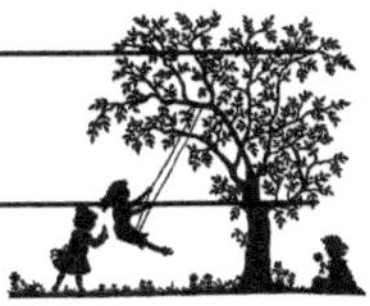

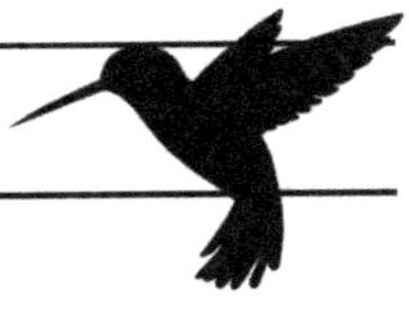

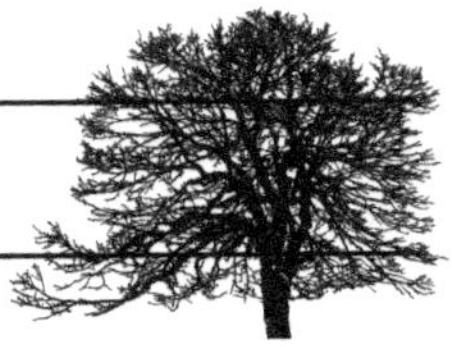

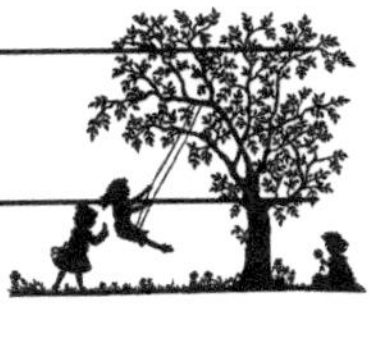

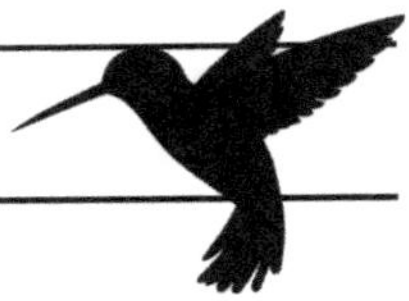

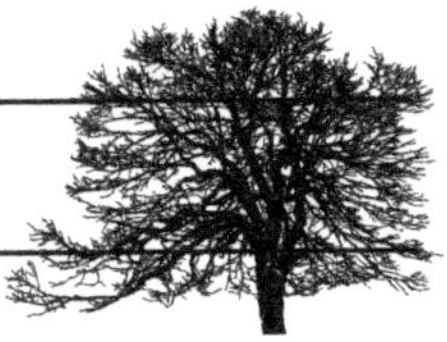

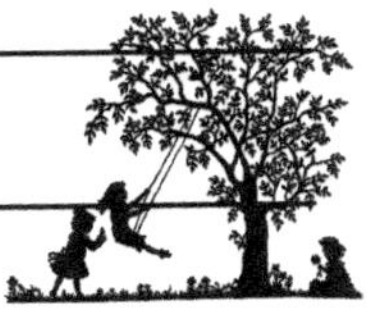

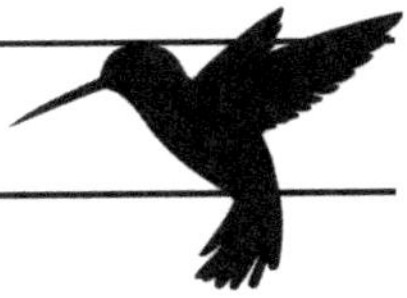

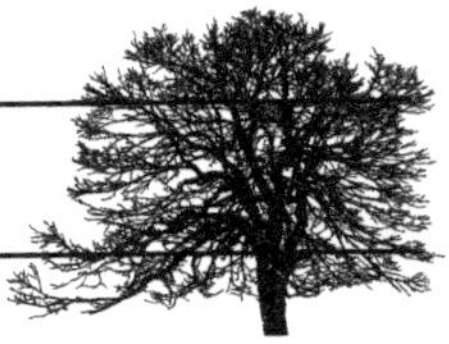

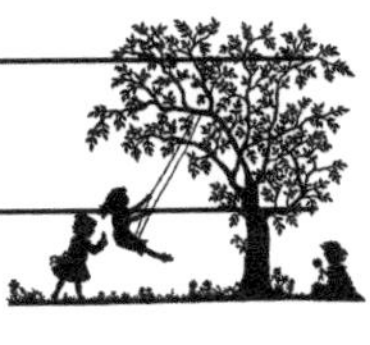

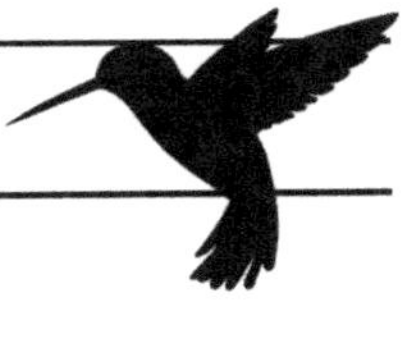

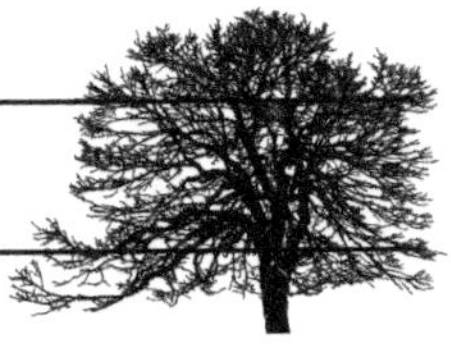

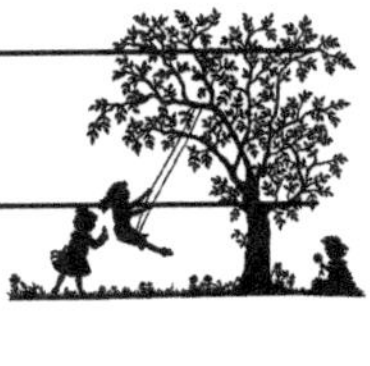

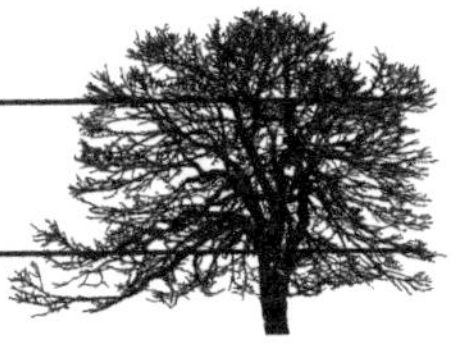

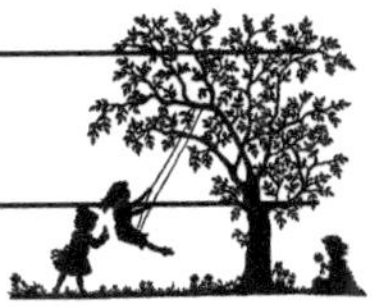

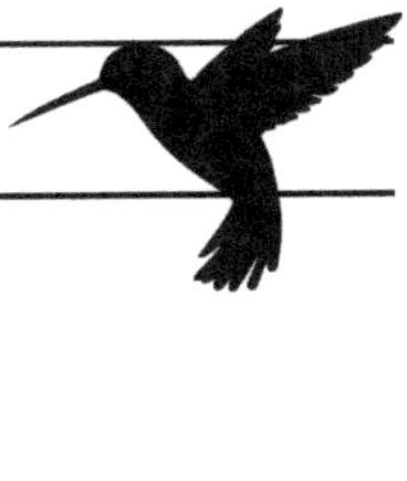

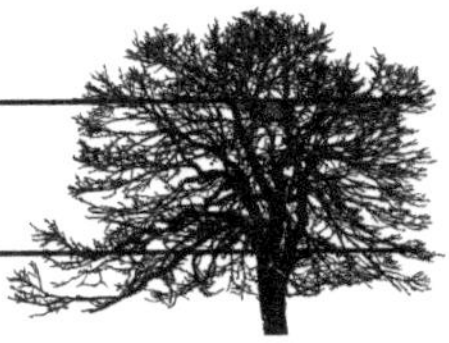

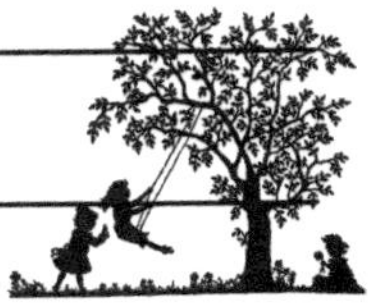

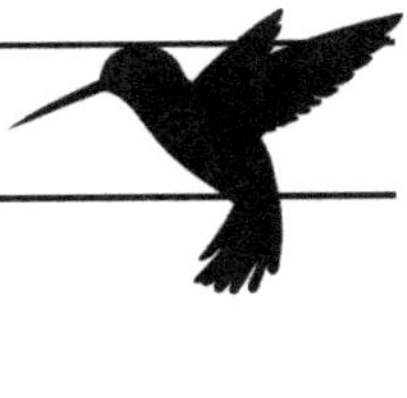

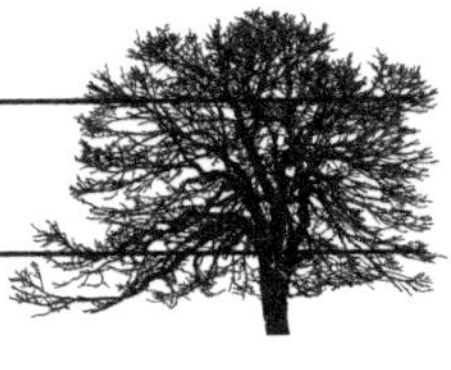

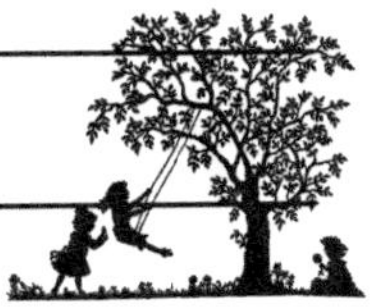

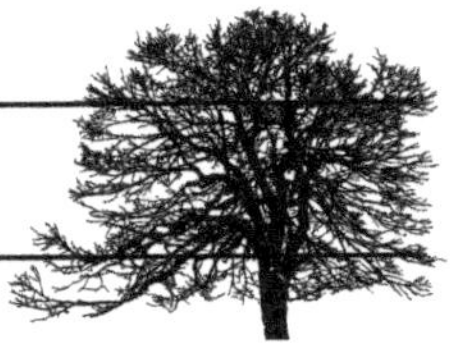

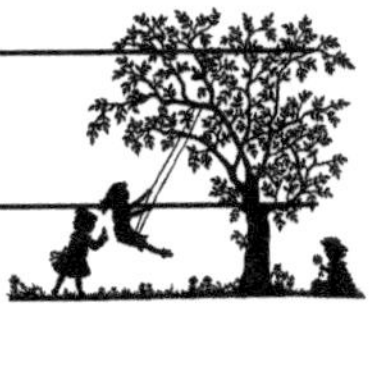

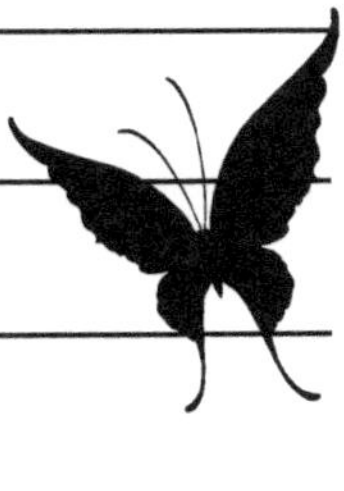

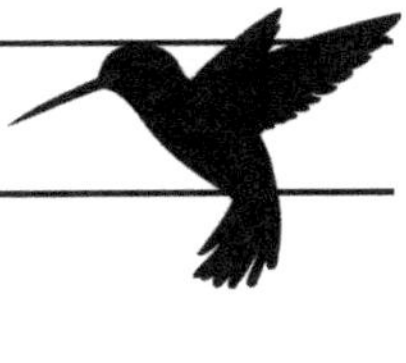

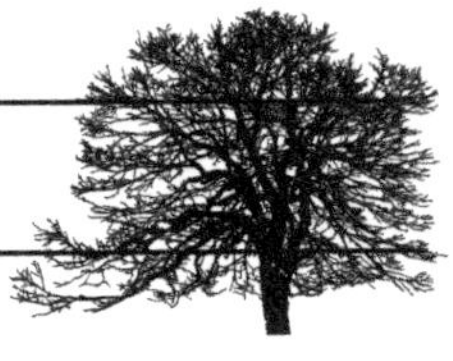

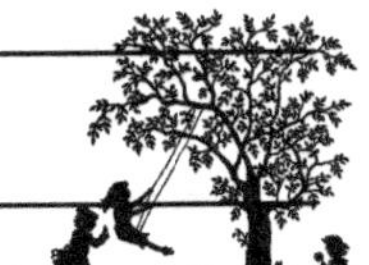

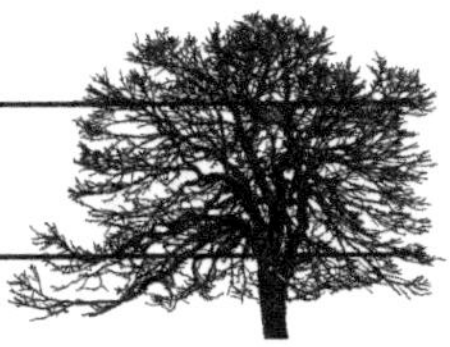

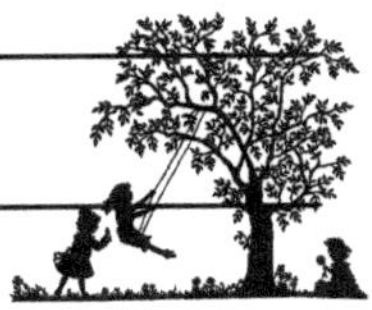

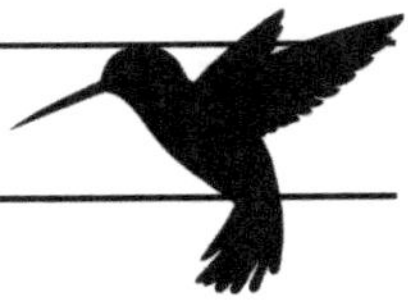

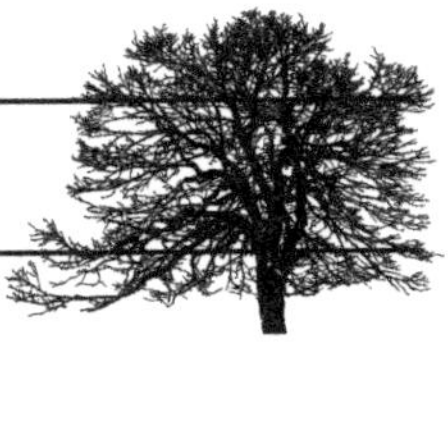

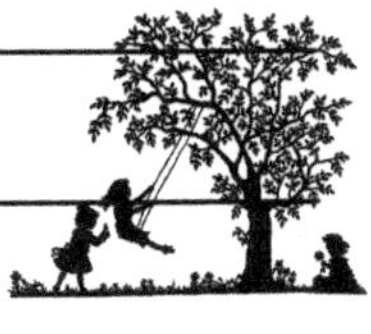

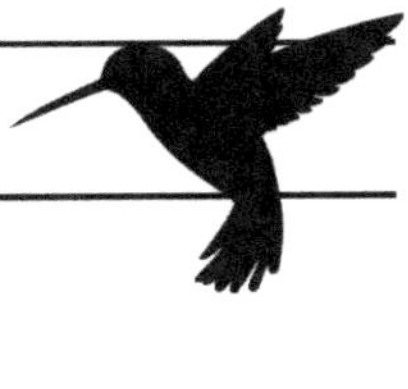

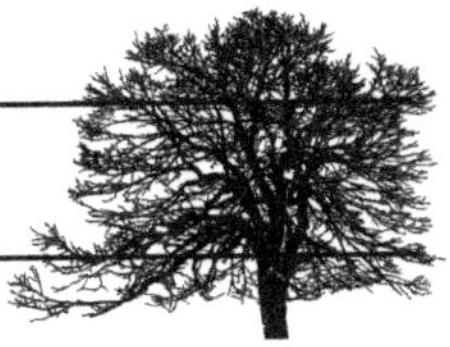

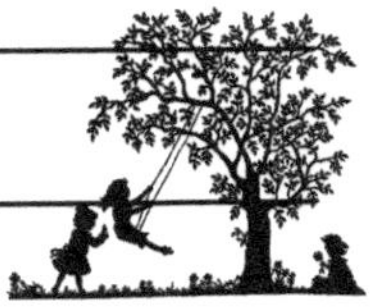

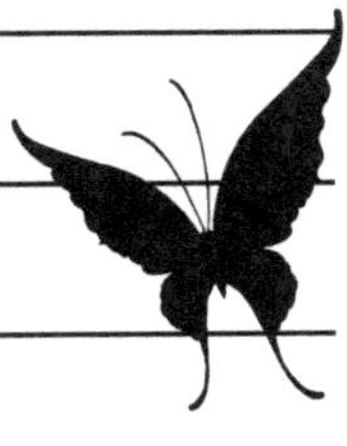

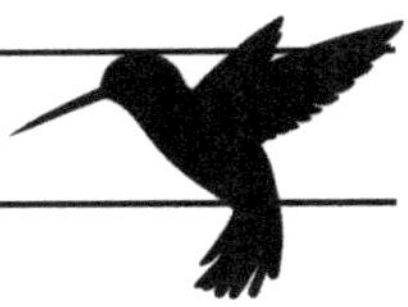

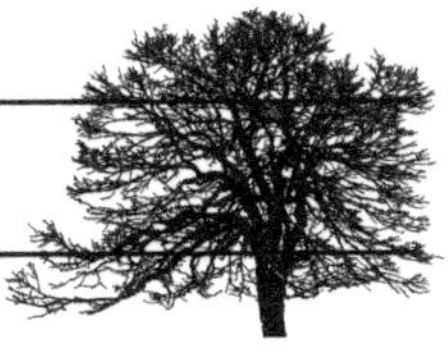

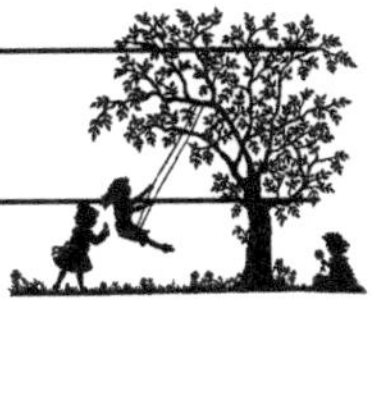

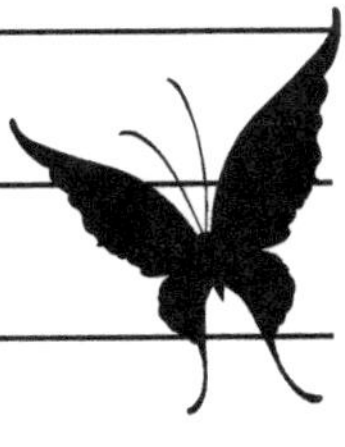

www.ingramcontent.com/pod-product-compliance
Lightning Source LLC
Chambersburg PA
CBHW072052280526
45788CB00006B/2263
* 9 7 8 1 0 9 1 1 6 1 0 0 9 *